# Writings For My Daughters

Taneet Grewal

BookLeaf Publishing

Writings For My Daughters © 2022 Taneet
Grewal

All rights reserved.


No part of this publication may be
reproduced, stored in a retrieval system, or
transmitted, in any form or by any means,
electronic, mechanical, photocopying,
recording or otherwise, without the prior
written permission of the presenters.


Taneet Grewal asserts the moral right to be
identified as author of this work.


Presentation by *BookLeaf Publishing*

Web: www.bookleafpub.com

E-mail: info@bookleafpub.com


ISBN: 978-93-95969-34-5

First edition 2022

# DEDICATION

For mothers and daughters everywhere

# ACKNOWLEDGEMENT

Thank you for believing in me
And helping me believe too

You know who you are

Sawubona
I love you

# PREFACE

"Each time a woman stands up for herself, without knowing it possibly, without claiming it, she stands up for all women."
– Maya Angelou

# Vomit

I watch
Heaving
As it swirls down
Disappears and
Leaves me alone
With the terrifying thought
That I am not alone

# Heartbeat

2

Birds
Symphonies
Oceans
Kirtan on a Sunday
Onions sizzling in oil
Mummy Daddy laughing together
Many wonderful sounds
That have kissed my ears
But none as beautiful
As the morning when
I first heard your heartbeat

# Flutter

You've probably been feeling some movement,
The doctor says.
I'm not sure,
I respond.
You know those butterflies in your tummy,
Faintly fluttering?
That, he says, is your baby.

# Honour

There are people in this world
Who throw out
Their babies
Like bags of garbage
Filled with broken dolls
Only because
Those babies
Are assigned the female gender
At birth.

In other parts of the world
People throw parties
And they call them
Gender reveal
They shoot out
Pink or Blue

In the country of my elders
And ancestors
They value the birth
Of baby boys
But even as I lay
In a Canadian hospital bed
There were some
Who could not hide
Their disappointment
At the birth of my firstborn child
A daughter

Disappointment
At my baby's lack
Of a penis

But I counted
Ten fingers
Ten toes
Two eyes
And a nose

A healthy and beautiful
Miracle

It was an honour
Carrying you
In my womb
And a privilege
Bringing you into this world

# Purple Slippers

Take my hand.
Do you feel the fingers
of the wind
running through your hair?
We'll become wild flowers
and dance against the summer air.

Take my hand.
Do you see the purple slippers
sparkling at your feet?
And the matching ballgown
we'll glide in when we meet
our faithful princes
who will treat us as their queens.

Take my hand.
Do you hear the music,
the song of that red bird?
We'll soar across the ocean
to hear of stories never heard.

Take my hand.
Please don't let go.
We're going to a land
where no one can say no.
Don't look back now.
The grown ups are gone.
Keep holding on now.
We're where we belong.

# Born

Light.
I can see.
My eyelashes flutter
rapidly
over and over and over again.
Cries.
I can hear.
A tiny voice inside me
grows
louder and louder and louder.
Thump-ump.
I can feel.
The beat rolls right through
Me.
Thump-ump, thump-ump, thump-ump,
Thump-ump.
A second beat.
Belongs not to me but to
You.
I can feel.
You.
The warmth
of your body
The warmth
from your eyes.
They look down
at me
and tell me

I belong.
to you
You belong
to me.
Life.
I can breathe.
My fingers hug your
finger
Tighter and tighter and tighter
Life.
I can breathe.
My body held close in your
embrace.
Forever and ever and ever.
I can see. I can hear. I can feel.
You:
My light. My cries. My beat.

# Phantom Kicks

I place my hand on my tummy where you once
lived
and still feel you dancing

This tummy that is covered in blazing stripes
soft like the atta we knead

Still feels your kicks and jumps
like a reel of film

Playing out the memories
perhaps never wanting
to let go

# Milk

When my baby cries
There is an ache in my breasts
It squeezes, it clenches
And then releases
As I place my baby against me
To latch on

The milk
It rushes out
Hurrying to get to
Her little mouth
So hungry

Then I switch from one side
To the other
Empty to full
Emptying me
Filling her

Somehow knowing this
Seeing her sleepy face
And milky lips
Hearing her burp
Fills up my heart
Like nothing else

# Brown Body

Once upon a time
I would look into the mirror
And imagine
My brown eyes turning blue
My black hair turning blonde
My soft curves becoming hard muscle
My short legs stretching out long and slender

Once upon a time
I didn't know who I was
So I did my best
To become someone else
Anyone other than me

It took many years
Much longer than it should have
For me to fall in love
With this beautiful brown skin
That my beautiful soul is wrapped in

Not to mention
The hips that held my babies
The breasts that fed them
The legs which kept me going
When I thought I could not stand
The mouth I use to read stories
Aloud
Every night at bedtime

"Once upon a time..."

# Your Sex

At a very tender age
I learned that my virginity
Was everything

It represented
My innocence
My purity
My dignity
My honour
My self-respect

For it to be taken
Before being married
Equated to the lowest form
Of disgrace

Once it is taken
Or given away
You can never
Ever
Get it back

And then you are left with
Nothing.

This only applies
If you have a
Vagina

I did not unlearn these beliefs
Until long after
The trauma of my
Sexual experiences
Had settled deep within
My core

You see,
Your sex
Belongs only
To you

It is not meant
For family, friends, acquaintances
Or strangers
To judge

Your virginity
Is not
Your identity

You decide
You choose
When it is time
And who it is with

Someone who cares
About your physical, mental
And emotional wellbeing
In a safe environment
With protection in
Every sense

It is not everything
It should not weigh you down

Carry yourself
Your self worth
As high as humanly
Possible

# Life is Now

I'm supposed to ask you
What you want to be
When you grow up.

Instead I ask you
Who do you want to be
Now?

Life is not about
Careers

Wiring young children
Into believing
They have to have it all
Figured out
Is wrong

Be free
In your days
Of youth

And when you become
An adult
You'll discover
None of us have it
Figured out

# Hairy Girl

Long ago in ancient Egyptian times,
Someone decided that humans
Must be hairless.

Soon this idea came to the West,
Advertising to females that they
Should be hairless.

Smooth, soft, touchable
Hair free
Legs, arms, underarms,
Face, fingers, toes,
Between the legs,
Between the cheeks,
Hair free.

Someone somewhere decided
We are more desirable
After we have used razors
To shave it off
After we have used wax
To rip if off

Making us appear
More feminine
More youthful
Like we are pre pubescent
Young children

Sexualized

Someone somewhere decided
We are unhygienic
If our skin is
Covered by our
Natural, God-given
Hair

If someone somewhere decided
We have to chop off
Our eyelashes
Would you do it?

You must be the someone
To decide
What beauty is

Whether you rock
A beard on your face
A bush down below
Or strands along your legs

You are worthy
You are beauty
You are divine
Femininity

Hairy girls
Are goddesses too.

# Queens

We straighten each other's crowns
We hold each other high
Arm in arm, allies.

We celebrate each other's wins
When she wins, you win, I win.

YAS honey
They call us queens
We will make our voices heard
We will make sure we are seen.

# BFFs

Not every mother
Gives birth to her best friend

Not every daughter
Gets a best friend in her mother

Somehow the planets and stars
All aligned

Somehow the sun and moon
The sky and earth
The oceans and rivers

The universe
in all Her immaculate power
Bestowed upon me
Two besties
in the form
of daughters.

# Language

When I went to preschool,
my teachers they would say:
"we don't understand your daughter"
to my parents.

For the mother tongue in which I spoke
so fluidly and fluently
was Punjabi.

We lived in a small city as a small family
your Nani and Nanu,
immigrants.

As the English language became
as familiar to me as Punjabi,
my cousins, they said,
"you're so white-washed."

They visited us in the small city
four hours away from their big city
where there were many
Punjabi speaking families.

As I grew older, so did my confusion
for my identity was never
quite right.

Never Canadian enough
Yet also never Indian enough.

# Mother

There once was a girl, seven years old
Whose mother died from poison,
Or so the story is told.

The girl grew up; angry, afraid
Of monsters and darkness,
And the shadows she made.

She married, had children, lived in despair
For she wished more than anything
That her mother was there.

The world was against her, or so she believed
Her body ached with agony, even with
Every prayer she weaved.

Her children married, had children, and lived in
despair
For their mother was unhappy
And her pain they could not bear.

She had three grandchildren, radiant and bright
They ran to her and hugged her
With all their might.

She looked at her children and grandchildren
The love that they shared, and realized then
Her mother had always been there.

# Reflection

When I am an old woman
I won't own a cane
I'll still wear my heels
and go dancing in the rain

When I am an old woman
I won't be a size one
I'll squeeze into that little Gucci dress
and sing 'girls just wanna have fun'

When I am an old woman
I'll play football in the park
and hold close my sweet grandkids
until the day turns dark.

When I am an old woman
I'll look into the mirror
I'll see someone who is happy
and who doesn't live in fear
of the day I'll be floating
up there in the clouds
I'll know I lived a life worth living
I'll know I made Her proud
Instead of getting, always giving

When I am an old woman
My heart will still be strong
I'll live each day through laughter
Until the day that I am gone.

# Holding You

Dirty dishes
are piled high in the sink

Heaps of laundry
in various corners of the house

Social media notifications
pinging on my phone

Pandemics and protests and propaganda
bursting on every news outlet

Patriarchy, misogyny and racism
are waiting on the doorstep

But I close my eyes
and I hold you

I will always hold you

www.ingramcontent.com/pod-product-compliance
Lightning Source LLC
LaVergne TN
LVHW021345200726
843509LV00014B/2674